Special Education
as a
Spiritual Journey

Michael Resman

——— Pendle Hill Pamphlet 390 ———

About the Author

Michael Resman is an occupational therapist who has served children and adults with developmental disabilities for thirty years. He is currently clerk of the Rochester (Minnesota) Friends Meeting and clerks the Northern Yearly Meeting Building Management Committee. In addition to providing support for the annual gathering of Friends General Conference, he has assisted in leading workshops at Pendle Hill.

Publications staff: Shirley Dodson
Pamphlet edited by Chel Avery and designed by Mary Helgesen Gabel
Requests for permission to quote or to translate should be addressed to:
Pendle Hill Publications, 338 Plush Mill Road, Wallingford, PA 19086-6023
Email: publications@pendlehill.org
Copyright © 2007 by Pendle Hill
ISBN 978-0-87574-390-5
June 2007

Special Education as a Spiritual Journey

The fruit of the Spirit is love, joy, peace, patience, kindness, generosity, faithfulness, gentleness, and self control.

(Galatians 5:22-23)

Introduction

Recently, I worked with a girl who was facing great adversity. In the period of eighteen months she had gone from being a healthy, gifted student to someone struggling with stroke-like symptoms, including impaired vision and a limited ability to speak. In response to questions she wrote out prompt and cogent phrases, so I knew she was fully alert and aware. Now that she had returned to school it was my task to support her independence.

I made arrangements for a different desk to be brought to the classroom so her wheelchair could fit under it. When I sat down next to her and explained the arrangements I had made, she pulled out her clipboard and wrote "bless you." I was deeply touched and had to hide my feelings to maintain my professional composure. I recognized that I had been blessed by an angel.

* * *

For more than twenty years, I have served children with disabilities as an occupational therapist in public schools. I have always been drawn to children with the most severe disabilities, including the apparent inability to speak or to understand words, limited vision, orthopedic and muscular problems which impede the ability to move, and multiple medical conditions. Some of my students occasionally "forget" to breathe, are unable to regulate their body temperature, and have life-threatening seizures. Their health may be very fragile, and hospitalizations are common. They may not recognize me, and some show no reaction to being touched or picked up. Many of my students are less severely affected, but I have always gravitated to those with the most needs.

Looking back over my career, I see that it was Grace that led me to these children. It took years before I began to understand what had attracted me to them. Having been a parentally-abused child, I entered adulthood wounded and afraid. Adding a native shyness and social awkwardness to these wounds, I was always guarded and closed when dealing with people. But I could give myself totally to these children without fear of being hurt or rejected. This was a very humble beginning based primarily on my limitations; but as I learned, God starts work with us as we are.

These children, whom many regarded as hopelessly retarded, became my teachers. That it took me a lifetime to learn is a reflection not of the quality of their teaching, but of my limited ability to comprehend and of the countless repetitions I required for some lessons to sink in.

Patience

When people first hear about what I do, they often comment, "You must have a lot of patience." I suggest instead that I have appropriate expectations. It is a huge advantage for me to be able to work one-on-one with children. Free of other distractions, we are able to attend to each other.

My responsibility is to help them learn to do things such as writing, cutting, dressing, and feeding themselves. I focus on the details of what they are doing. Who would not celebrate if a child could double her output? For me, that can mean cutting for an inch instead of only half an inch. If I expected them to cut like their age peers, I would be frustrated and impatient. How silly. In our little corner the child and I can do things her way, and celebrate each tiny accomplishment.

Years ago I led a team that taught a young adult to feed himself. For twenty-one meals a week we all set up his place exactly as he needed it, providing him with precisely the amount of assistance he needed but no more, as he went through the steps to independence. It took three years of problem solving, communicating, and cooperating to support him through that process. I will always look at my work with that team as a high point in my career. Patience? It was a requirement of the job, opening the door to other experiences.

* * *

Poetry is one of the ways I seek to find meaning in my life and work. The following poem was written in 1982, before I had children, and years before my spiritual opening. I was emotionally attached to my students, but had perhaps invested too much self-worth in my ability to produce improvements in their condition. Lacking a deeper perspective, I revolved around pity—for them and myself.

PITY

Are you well enough
to smile at me today?
When you do, our crib lights up,
and I don't notice
the tube that's in your nose.
Your soft cheeks dimple,
and emotions rush
to crowd behind my eyes.
I wish, how I wish.
But that won't bring a change.
What good are feelings.
What good am I.
I can't help you.

Gentleness

When people have tight muscles and do not fully move some part of their body, they may develop contractures—a shortening of the muscles and connective tissue. Soon they are no longer able to bend or straighten the affected joints fully. Part of my job is to prevent these contractures and reverse them, if possible, by restoring movement.

For the first few years I practiced as I was taught. I stretched tightened joints by carefully placing my hands, aligning the joint and firmly pulling. The children found this uncomfortable and resisted. As a result of my zeal to provide excellent care during my first years, two of my students had to be seen at the emergency room because I stretched their ankles too vigorously.

I was ignoring what was happening right in front of me and was oblivious to the consequences of my actions. Influenced by my training, I was intruding with some violence on these vulnerable lives. I did not realize that, because they were sore after I finished, their muscles often tightened even more in the following hours.

After the first incident of using too much force, I resolved to be more careful. A year later, when a child moved unexpectedly and I again stressed an ankle, I resolved to stop using any force to accomplish my goals. Instead, I studied massage and practiced positioning the children's joints in ways that they found relaxing. When I straightened out their joints after relaxing them I was gentle and slow.

Several of the children were unable to use their trunk muscles to breathe normally. Rather than lifting and expanding their ribs to inhale, their ribs stayed still. The only movement I could see was from their diaphragm, their bellies going in and out markedly with each breath. I tried everything I could think of to awaken, strengthen, and position the muscles of their upper trunks to help with breathing. I never found anything that would help very much.

The process of spending weeks closely attending to their breathing opened levels of learning I had not known existed. The children were leading, and my task was to focus and follow. Because they needed such specialized and large equipment, I usually worked with the students in their special education classroom. These busy, noisy places are typically distracting, particularly when multiple adults are exchanging information. I learned to tune all the noise out and focus for long periods on the child I was holding.

After months, I discovered that I was matching my breathing and heart rate more closely to the child's. I developed a practice that I use to this day: at the beginning of each session I approach the child, and while looking at him face to face, I put my hand lightly on his chest. I just sit, with my hand on his chest, and we gaze at each other for a minute while I work to synchronize with him.

Gradually I grew aware that I was communicating with my hands. These mute children were communicating with me, and I with them, through touch. I learned first to read their physical status and later their mood with my hands. This joyful, awe-inspiring discovery process went on for years until it became part of who I am professionally. Over the years, I have attended workshops, learning how to gently help connective and muscle tissues to soften and glide.

Tammy

I remember sunlight on fine golden hair
freckles sprinkled on nose and cheek
eyes that sparkled when I approached
a smile that warmed the room
it wasn't easy keeping up
with a perfect child
so many things I got from you
did I give back equal measure?
the things you taught will stay with me
to use with other kids
more patient, kind, responsible
you made us better people
I'm going to miss your gentle sigh
the way you moved about
my arms you see are empty now
God speed, little angel

Love

Now that I was working on opening myself and connecting deeply, and was doing things with the children rather than to them, I found that I had moved from a professional concern to a deep love for each child. I did not talk about these attitudes with my colleagues. They set high standards, and the highest was professional detachment, which was supposed to help us to be objective.

I did not care to be detached. I wanted to revel in the love I felt for each child. I found that I could still remain objective, making judgments that were perhaps even more appropriate, because I looked deeper into the life circumstances not just of the children, but also of their parents and caregivers.

Children often responded to my efforts to relax their tight muscles by smiling and waving their arms and legs more freely. It was clear that the students enjoyed having me work with them and that I was enjoying each session as well. The loving feelings I carried were obvious but unspoken. Other staff who had themselves bonded closely with the children were grateful for my efforts, and we formed an unspoken conspiracy, our emotional connections to the children connecting us to each other as well.

Alone in my office and at home I pondered these children's conditions. Some were in great pain. Others had to endure repeated surgeries. I was troubled by the question of justice. How could a loving God allow these obviously innocent children to suffer?

My casual childhood exposure to several Protestant denominations and the Catholic Church did not provide an answer. It was clear to me that the children changed the lives of all those who knew them. The deepest meaning I could come up with for the children's conditions was the growth

I could see in their caregivers. But for the innocent to suffer without recompense so that others could learn and grow was monstrous, unthinkable. I had always heard that God was good and caused no evil. Then where was God in the lives of the children I served? For years, I chewed on my questions, circling round and round without reaching any understanding.

Some of my religious beliefs from childhood began to change. I came to see that my lowest-functioning students were perfect children, who spent their lives without ever doing anything wrong. I questioned the notion of original sin and the need for baptism. I felt privileged to be working with these perfect beings.

Some of the children were medically fragile, and on average a current or former student of mine has died each year. No matter what the religious denomination, during their funerals the most frequent answer to the children's lives given by the religious leader was, "God's purposes are unknowable." That did not satisfy me. I cared too much to accept a non-answer.

After about ten years of this work, I went looking for a Sunday school for my older daughter. I found my way to a Quaker meeting, and immediately felt that I had arrived at a spiritual home. During the next six months, I worked to connect with God, and slowly learned to make use of the silence.

I came to revere a couple who epitomized a mature Quaker spirituality. When the woman was severely injured in a car accident, my spiritual world came crashing down. During meeting for worship the next Sunday, I demanded an answer from God about why God allowed this terrible injustice to happen to such a kind, loving servant. All the years of pain and frustration I was carrying from my childhood and the lives of the children I served was heaped on. "Why?" I demanded of God. "Why?"

In response, I was lifted to heaven, and was fully in the presence of God. Those sitting next to me in meeting for worship had no idea that anything had occurred, but during that period, which lasted perhaps ten minutes, my life was utterly changed.

God's love overwhelmed me. It was as if all the love every mother had for her children across the world and throughout history had been gathered and given to me. I was surrounded, immersed in, permeated by Love. I felt comforted and grateful beyond words and came away from the experience with only two truths—that God is perfect love, and that heaven is forever. These were very simple concepts, but now they are the basis of my life.

I had to rethink everything I had believed from this new viewpoint—from the perspective of heaven. A divine presence that I came to know as "Holy Spirit, Mother" was with me constantly for the next six months, comforting and teaching me. I no longer believed, I *knew* that God existed. More clearly than my senses are able to teach me about the realities of this life, I had experienced a truth that changed the core of my being. My soul would live forever in the presence of God, and I live from moment to moment in God's palm, surrounded by love and grace.

This opening was difficult for me to process. I have since learned that epiphany experiences occur across religions, and that what was happening to me was a form of mysticism—direct experiences of God. At the time, however, I was afraid that others would question my sanity. I had no one to turn to for advice. I struggled with my interior life in silence for about six months. Writing poetry helped me process what was happening.

As part of applying for membership in my meeting, I shared the opening I had received and the ongoing process I was experiencing. I was deeply grateful when my meeting responded with warm acceptance. I had feared that they might say my beliefs were unwelcome. One member told me that Quakerism is a mystical religion, and my epiphany experience was uncommon, but within that tradition. My focus on heaven was not shared by many Quakers. While my beliefs were different from those of others in my meeting, differing beliefs among members were in keeping with Quaker practice. My meeting warmly supported my efforts to deepen my spiritual life in my own way.

In time Northern Yearly Meeting developed a spiritual nurture program, consisting of two annual retreats and smaller local groups that met regularly. I eagerly joined and attended retreats for several years. A small group of us from my meeting have met monthly for many years. Our format includes an opportunity for each of us to share an update of our spiritual condition. As I developed understandings I shared them with the group, along with my successes and frequent shortcomings in applying these understandings to my outward life. The expectation of regular, deep sharing with this group has served to hold me accountable.

I learned another way of knowing—I found that deeper than the intellect or emotions, there is a spiritual awareness capable of consuming huge truths and arriving at new Truth in an instant. These quick insights came to me during visions, where I was given openings that I absorbed as a whole. The visions helped me remember, keeping the experience vivid while I pondered what I had learned. Whipsawed between humility at my poor condition and spiritual ecstasy, I stumbled forward.

At the same time, I was practicing a slower method of learning—holding up an issue and examining it from the new perspectives I had been given. I thus developed two levels of understanding. It was certainly possible that I may have misunderstood a truth I had received during a vision. These understandings were given whole. My task was to take them in and remember. In turn, I took these new insights and applied them, sometimes to things I had thought I had understood and believed, and sometimes to things I had never understood.

I brought my concern about the inherent injustice in the lives of my students to this slower process and spent several years pondering my questions. First I saw that we all existed before we were born, nurtured in the heart of God. It became a foundation of my life that our time in this world is short and illusory. Our true, permanent home is heaven. I developed a deep longing for a return to my real home.

I recognized that my life view had changed. I had held a vague assumption that there was life after death, but notions of heaven were not important or relevant to my daily life. Now, returning and spending forever in heaven was the central reality of my earthly life.

I examined the lives of my students against this background. It came to me that we all agree to the circumstances of our lives before we are born. The central concerns of our earthly lives are the choices we make, for we have freedom to live as we wish within our circumstances.

Some of us are fortunate, growing up with health, loving parents, peace, adequate resources, and abilities. Some are born with few or none of these advantages. The challenge—the opportunity—for those of us who have much is to give to those who have little. Gradually, I focused on the importance of need.

What would the world be like if no one were in need? At first blush, this condition sounds ideal. What if no one were ever sick physically or mentally, what if children cared for and taught themselves, and what if everyone always felt happy? There would be no need for health care workers, teachers, or parents. Friendships would not include helping or comforting, for each of us would be self-sufficient. What a self-centered, limited existence that would be!

Many of us could not be fulfilled, could not be complete persons, without participating in giving.

In this earthly life God has granted us freedom, and we have many choices. The most holy choice is to seek a relationship with God. Such a relationship will lead to a life of service. This service can be as abstract as praying for others or as concrete as being a janitor. For any of us to serve there must be people in need.

Where is the justice for those who live in great need? There is none in this world. One school year, after witnessing our students go through many painful situations, my colleagues and I developed a shorthand for "Life Isn't Fair"—LIF. When circumstances in the classroom became difficult, or when we became distressed about what a student was going through, the staff would comfort each other by saying, "Just give it a LIF."

There is only justice in the next world, where God honors those who lived in need. It was their need that provided the opportunities for those around them to grow in holiness. The greater the needs, the greater the opportunities. This is an answer for why God allows the innocent to suffer. The pain experienced in this fleeting transitory existence is salved by God's particular love—for eternity. What cannot be understood or answered in this world is transformed into joy in the next.

I shared my belief that we agree to the circumstances of our lives and my understanding of the importance of need with my spiritual nurture group. I was cautioned that these beliefs can be misused to place blame or withhold care. I took that caution to heart and looked deeply and carefully.

I saw that lurking within the human psyche is a tendency to project blame. "They must have done something to deserve their circumstances" is an all-too-frequent belief. This mechanism serves well to protect us. We are assured that the same things will not befall us, for we do not deserve them. We are also excused from extending or sacrificing ourselves to provide meaningful service. After all, those people are simply getting their just desserts. Taken to an extreme, it could be said that this suffering must be God's will, and to interfere would be wrong.

A concomitant belief is that these people must be inferior to us. Measured by the world's values of beauty, wealth, talent, and accomplishment, surely we have done—surely we *are*—far better than they. Most of us are aware that we are born with the privileges and abilities that make our accomplishments possible and would deny holding such an arrogant posture. But it is an easy stance to slip into when the alternative is to live fully into the consequences of considering those who are disabled, mentally ill, impoverished, or deprived as our peers in worthiness.

A focus on the meaning of need turns this shallow belief system on its head. Those in need provide the opportunities for others to grow in the only thing spiritually important—the most worthy goal of this life, holiness, living in harmony with the will of God. Viewed through the eyes of heaven, those most in need—the homeless, difficult, poor, and ill among us and throughout the world—may be leading lives more in tune with God's will than are we.

STONE TRAVEL

If you would know the universe
travel through a stone.
Feel its borders from within
taste its minerals.
Inventory atoms,
recalling where each has been.
Then you will find
outside the bounds,
the center.
And you will know
we are one
and have been
before time
before space
and shall be one again
after we account
for where we've been.

Kindness

Several years after my spiritual opening I was assigned to assist a kindergartner in transitioning from a mental health day treatment program into the public schools. I made several trips to the treatment center to learn about him from the staff and to meet him. He was a small, disordered, extraordinarily fearful child.

In order to develop some trust, I sat on the floor next to him and played some games. As I often do, I frequently asked him for help in figuring out how the games worked. Helping me—an apparently confused, ignorant adult—quickly engaged him and boosted his confidence. This approach, combined with focusing on him in a quiet, calm manner, seemed to make him comfortable with me.

Careful transportation arrangements were made for his first day at school. He would be the only student on a small bus. Staff would be waiting at the door to meet the bus and lead him to class.

The child would be attending my home school, but I was assigned to travel to a different school that morning and return for a session with this child later in the day. I packed my therapy equipment on that first day, left the building, and got about a mile away before remembering something I had to have. Muttering at my stupidity I returned, parking in the back lot of the school. As I walked up the sidewalk, I saw the student from the day treatment center standing near the door and looking utterly forlorn. He had been dropped off at the wrong door!

I knelt down, greeted him, and then led him to his classroom. Afterward, as I gathered up my forgotten materials and drove across town, I marveled at what had happened. God had used me, without my knowledge. Moreover, God had made use of my mistake to carry out an act of mercy.

I had been assuming that I must strive for perfection in order to be worthy and capable of serving God. Here I was seeing the opposite. It was my limitations that had provided an opening for me to be used.

I pondered further, seeking to understand what I should do, if I accepted that I did not need to be perfect to serve God.

Two principles I was already struggling with emerged in my mind—obedience and trust in God. If these practices resulted in a good heart, God could make use of me, faults and all. It has been a great comfort in my life to know that I do not have to be perfect, because God can make use of my limitations.

There have been a number of other instances where, in looking back, I can see that God has moved me here or there in order to make use of me. I had mistakenly assumed that I would be asked whether I was willing to do a particular service, but instead the opportunities to serve simply emerged in my path.

During one of the annual gatherings of Friends General Conference, I decided (seemingly at random) to sit on a bench in front of the dining hall after eating breakfast. I was helping to lead a workshop for which I was carrying a boom box. While I was sitting, idly enjoying the flower bed in front of me, a woman walked up and asked whether she could use the boom box that afternoon for a presentation. I agreed, and we made arrangements for me to leave it in a certain room after lunch.

After she walked away, a voice that I recognized as God's said to me, "You can get up now." I understood in an instant that God had moved me to sit on the bench and her to walk by at that same moment. It is miraculous and rather frightening to realize that what I often believe is "my" life can be taken over by God without my knowledge or consent.

That same afternoon, as I was leaving the building where we had agreed I should leave the boom box, I met the woman coming in. I related to her the voice I had heard and my interpretation that God was lovingly supporting her presentation. She seemed touched and reassured.

I walked away, shaking my head in wonder that it had happened once again. God had moved the two of us so we would meet. Now when seemingly random coincidences occur, I remind myself to stop and seek out whether God is at work. Often I do not know what is going on, and have to be content with not knowing.

Dance

I could want nothing more
than to dance in the palm of God.
Surrounded by Friends
whose tender concern
lifts me.
To go forth in Love-lit mist
seeing dimly, but forever.
My ear turned
inward
outward
and I know
and knowing leap yes!
Yes.
Dazed by the touch of forgiveness
I wander through the world.

Generosity

As I gained expertise in helping with children's sensory needs, I was asked by parents to help them at home with serious issues like children's not eating or sleeping. I was willing to do this for my students, but with my own family responsibilities, I was not interested in developing a second job.

These consultations would require multiple visits. The first time I went to a house, I asked the parents to describe the problem and viewed the environment. I made suggestions and developed plans with the parents, then several weeks later I returned to see how well the plans had worked. With these complex children the first plans rarely worked satisfactorily. We would make improvements to our approach, and I would return in several weeks.

After a first visit, parents usually wanted to pay me before I left. I was not working for the money, and in the beginning I refused any payment. I noticed, however, that this skewed my relationship with the parents. I sensed that they were reluctant to call me if they had questions or problems between scheduled sessions, and they limited the number of visits. In some cases, plans were not followed. I could not be sure whether the plans had been inappropriate, or if my suggestions were not being valued because, after all, they were free. How valuable could these services be if the practitioner was willing to give them away?

I resolved to accept $10.00 per visit if asked by a parent what I charged. This was a small fraction of what an in-home visit by an occupational therapist would normally cost. This charge seemed to satisfy parents, as it created the typical client-provider roles. I smiled to myself when it worked so well that a few parents attempted to take advantage of the situation, requesting more visits than I thought were necessary.

I encountered the same phenomenon while working as a crew leader for Habitat for Humanity. People were uncomfortable receiving help without being able to reciprocate. When homeowners pressed on me ethnic foods that I could not identify or diet soda that I did not like, I realized that I needed to accept their gifts gracefully. Accepting from those I was helping completed the interaction, leaving both of us satisfied.

Giving, for many people, is a selfish activity in the sense that it provides multiple potential rewards to the giver. Unless the giving is mutual and equal, the giver attains some measure of status and power. Whether it is intended or not, an inherent part of providing help is putting the recipient in a subordinate position.

Issues of generosity between people pale when compared to God's generosity. The notion that God will reward us has been much used and abused. How sad that some religious leaders have pitched this reward in commercial terms, diverting people's efforts from far more important spiritual and emotional possibilities.

When I was captain of a Habitat for Humanity house, there were many details that demanded my attention. I always arrived early on work days to get things organized. After a time I resolved to come earlier still, so I could first pray for fifteen minutes, asking God to bless our work and keep us safe. The simple act on my part—disciplining myself to sit and center down while surrounded with tasks that needed doing—was hugely rewarded, for God granted me the gift of serenity. In all parts of my life, I began to develop a sense of calm. Rarely talked of or striven for, serenity is one of life's greatest gifts. I continued to be beset by problems and disappointments, but now could see over them. They had no claim on my emotions, and I could acknowledge them and let go. What a huge gift, all out of proportion to my meager effort!

Several years later, I attended a spiritual nurture program. Part of that process was choosing daily spiritual disciplines. I chose gratitude. During my daily prayers and as often as I could during the day, I gave thanks for whatever was in front of me, striving to see God's hand in my opportunities. Stopping for a red light provided a chance to pray. Difficult co-workers provided a challenge to grow in understanding and love.

After several weeks of working to be grateful, I was surprised that joy was growing deep in my heart. Not the exuberant jumping around kind of joy, but an awareness that all was well with the world and that I had nothing to fear. I was later to learn an even greater joy, but this joyous gratitude was another example of the great bounty I was given for a small effort.

These gifts were not given because of great accomplishments on my part, but in response to my tenuous and imperfect reaching toward God. I wanted to dance in the streets and shout about the great gifts available through a spiritual life, but I had no words and no leading to do so.

Vis

If invisible,
I could serve as window
to the other side.
With nonbeing,
a door.

Peace

After I had learned something of the spiritual basis underlying my work, one of my younger students died unexpectedly in her sleep. The grief of her family was deep and palpable, and was joined by the sorrow of school staff and her classmates.

During her funeral I was able to center deeply. I watched and was awed as her soul ascended to heaven. The entire universe joined in cheering, celebrating her life and return. The stark contrast between the joy I saw with my spiritual eyes and the grief surrounding me in the church wounded me, but there were no words that would comfort these people who knew me only slightly in a professional role. I hugged close to me the knowledge of how wondrously these children are watched and loved from heaven.

During the funerals that followed I found opportunities to be still and pray, working to connect with my students' departing souls. I watched as child after child joyfully slipped into heaven. One child who had had hydrocephalus floated over the worshipers as a butterfly before leaving.

Special education directors came and went. One was particularly difficult to work for, negatively affecting the entire department. I struggled to maintain my equilibrium and stay focused on students. When a child died that year, his funeral was much like the others had been. During my daily prayer several days later, my eyes were drawn to heaven, where I saw him. He was praying for me. Now he was helping care for all those who had cared for him, particularly his parents.

I drew great comfort when I saw that I would spend eternity surrounded by my students. While contemplating my celestial connections with students during subsequent prayers, I came to understand that I would spend eternity with everyone whom I had helped, hurt, hated, and loved.

Looking more broadly, I saw that everyone on earth is connected spiritually. There is no "us" and "them," no "I" and "not I," there is only "we." I was drawn to the suffering of children in the third world and saw that I would also spend eternity with souls I had ignored and neglected.

I had been taught as a child to fear God's judgment after death. I saw that this notion is entirely too narrow. God as perfect love gives us mercy, not justice. If the only thing we received from God were justice, there would be no hope for most of us.

Instead, I believe what we need to fear after death is our own judgment. When the scales fall from our eyes, we will be faced for eternity with the pitiful use we made of the great gifts God gave us. As humans we have an almost infinite capacity for self-deception, readily justifying almost any of our actions. In heaven we will see the broad, full effects of our behavior and will be stunned by the far-reaching consequences we have set in motion.

An act of kindness as small as a smile will be seen with the blessings it set off, contrasted to the suffering we caused by an unkind remark. The consequences of the self-absorption that is such a part of human nature will be clear. We will be faced with the thousands of opportunities we had to be merciful, but instead acted with selfishness or indifference.

The central reality of heaven is our soul's full exposure to God. What an incredible promise, to be so totally loved for eternity. But few of us deserve to spend forever in bliss after leading deeply flawed lives. While God's love and mercy will surround and permeate us, becoming our central reality, we will also grieve over our failures to make good use of the freedom we enjoyed while we were alive.

Only those who never chose wrongly will live in undiluted joy. My previous understanding that I was working with children who were leading perfect lives was reinforced.

DOVE

Sacred Dove,
come,
drink from my soul.
I would be a pool
still
pure enough
for you to bathe.
Letting failures,
all outcomes sink,
what can I rise up
for your splashing?
My gifts,
You gave.
I am,
was Yours.
Let us share sunbeams,
a single graceful note,
baby's soft caress.
Alone
unmoving
my life's task fulfilled
if You can bathe and rest.

Faithfulness

I resolved to pray more faithfully, to be more attentive to how God was leading me, and to give more generously to organizations working in third world countries.

One afternoon I laid a small boy on his back, in preparation for a session of relaxation. He was a happy child, despite his pipe-stem arms and legs and badly distorted chest. It took a few minutes to arrange the pillows around and under him so he would be comfortable, a necessary condition if he was going to be able to relax.

I remember that it was a sunny day, the light streaming down on him from the windows set high in the wall. As I bent over and gazed at him, his face suddenly changed, and I was looking into the face of Jesus. This was Jesus, come to earth again, as complete and real as I would ever know.

The visions I had experienced before had all occurred when I was praying with my eyes closed. This was happening while I was fully alert and had my eyes open.

In a moment, Jesus was gone, and the child was back with me, smiling into my eyes. I knew—I had been shown—the holiness of this child. By the world's standards, he was unimportant—unable now or in the future to work, walk, talk, or care for himself. In heaven's terms, he was a much beloved son.

There are no words to describe how that vision happened. None of the other staff in the room was aware that anything had occurred. I look back years later in wonder and give thanks for the blessing I received.

Several years ago, I prayed with a woman twenty-four hours after she had donated a kidney. With my spiritual eyes, I "saw" her wings—she was an angel. Later, during meeting for worship, I saw that my fellow worshipers had wings.

Looking further, I understood that we all have wings. Our earthly condition includes the possibility that we can serve as angels—agents of God's mercy.

Looking at my students, I saw that they were angels too. They had made their decision to lead lives in need and were agents of mercy, providing opportunities for others to grow.

Looking more at those around me, I saw the freedom that God grants us. The wings diminish on those who choose to accumulate wealth, power, and status for their personal ends. The wings grow on those who choose to pick up the tasks God lays before them.

End of My Sleeves

I looked at the end of my
sleeves
and there I saw God's hands.
I'd been wondering for years
how God's work would ever get done.
I see these hands came equipped
with arms and eyes and mind and heart.
Now, to sink this will in That One
and yet again, bring God on earth.

Self Control

Despite all the blessings I had been given, I remained deeply wounded from my dysfunctional childhood.

In response to an increasing need, the school district opened several classrooms for elementary-aged students with autism. Those first years with autistic students were difficult, as we struggled to develop techniques that would support them.

These were very disordered children. They had limited language skills and rigid, severe needs. Only five and six years old, many of them frequently became very upset, screaming, crying, and striking out at people and objects. I was hit, kicked, bitten, or scratched on a daily basis. Each time it happened, an emotional response ignited in me.

I was still carrying a lot of anger from having been physically abused as a child by my mother. The students' aggression tapped into that anger. Over and over again, I had to constrain myself in order to respond to a student in a measured, professional manner. Each child had a behavior plan, and it was essential for all of the staff to respond consistently.

It was not enough for me to avoid losing my temper; the expectation was that I would respond in a sophisticated manner. The effort involved in controlling my feelings was exhausting, and I was thankful that I worked only part time in those rooms.

I had always seen myself as a consummate professional who cared about others. Needing to struggle in order not to strike out at children did not fit that image. I mentally explored their behavior, my responses, and my dissatisfaction with myself. Being a slow learner, I struggled in this distressing condition for over two years. Finally, during a day-long prayer walk in a state park, I laid it before God. I asked for help, acknowledging that I could not find my way out of the situation I was in.

Pondering again the children's behavior and my response, I was led to look deeper within myself. I saw the huge well of anger I was carrying. It was understandable that I would be angry at my past mistreatment. I walked, my eyes open to the beauty of the park that surrounded me. I sat and prayed with my eyes closed, seeking to see as far as I could.

I was so tired from having to stifle my anger. God nudged me to look at forgiveness. I had set my feelings aside enough to have an adult relationship with my mother that was superficially functional. I had worked at forgiveness in the past, knowing that it was the "right" thing to do, but had not accomplished much.

I desperately wanted things to be different but still could see no way out. I walked some more, then settled again in prayer. I was led to sit with my anger, then to look below it, keeping in mind my unhappiness.

I looked at my mother's circumstances with an open heart. I knew that she had been mistreated as a child, and I had observed that she had few coping strategies as an adult. Sighing and clutching for spiritual support, I looked back at her while she was being abusive. I saw how the anger that she was carrying had spilled out, mixing with the rigid expectations she was holding about what others might think of her.

I sat, clinging to God's arms, and looked. Understanding and accepting her circumstances allowed me to let go of my anger. Forgiveness flowed out of me toward this woman of thirty years ago, and if not love, then acceptance of who she was and her efforts to do her best.

I got up and began walking again, dazed by what had happened in that instant. I shook my head and looked around. Was it true? Had I really forgiven her, and was the anger truly gone? I searched my feelings as I walked along.

Yes, it was true. I wondered whether it would make a difference and looked forward to my next session in the autism classrooms.

I was disappointed. I found myself responding in much the same way. But after several weeks I discovered that there was a difference. More and more often, I found I was responding more calmly, with detachment and even humor. After a year of practicing new habits, I discovered that the children's aggression no longer triggered anger within me, and I could respond in a measured, thoughtful manner.

Others have come to forgiveness more easily. I am grateful that the children supplied the stimulant which so stressed my view of myself that finally, in my exhaustion, I was able to lay this deep part of myself in God's lap and was open enough to see my abuser's condition.

All of Me

Come.
Come on, come on, come on, come on.
I would gather you under my arms;
good and evil,
life and death,
love and hatred.
I love thee,
I am thee.

Joy

Over the years, I came to say to myself that I wanted to live not merely a life of prayer, but life as a prayer. Of course I had to admit that I would only be able to do this for brief moments at a time, but it seemed like a worthy goal. I often prayed for the chance to do some big magnificent thing that would greatly improve the condition of the world.

That did not happen. I was led instead to focus on the tasks in front of me. I came to see my work with students as my vocation, in the religious sense. This viewpoint comes particularly to mind when people criticize the "Godless" public schools. If only I could tell them about the prayer that goes on in public schools and how God has led some of us to be where we are, doing what we do for children.

One of my hobbies is woodworking, and I have built numerous pieces of equipment for my students. One year I was asked to design and build a chair and some steps up to a sink for a child who was very short. She could walk and had normal intelligence, but she was unable to do some things because school environments were not set up for someone her size.

I was captivated by this tiny person and immediately resolved to do whatever I could to assist her. After carefully measuring her and the sink, I went back home to my workshop and set to work drawing.

I was at peace and very happy during the hours it took to design, build, and finish her furniture. Using all of my skills as a woodworker and therapist, I felt deeply centered. All of me was engaged in her service. For that time I had become a prayer. I was totally right with God and blissfully happy.

I had discovered heaven on earth. I first had to accept my aches and pains, parenting concerns, and frustrations with administrators—all the circumstances I found myself in. Heaven on earth is not found by the world being just as we would like it to be, but in accepting and therefore transcending whatever we face.

It is not required—and not guaranteed—that our efforts will result in success. We do not have to be wonderfully skilled. What is asked is what any of us could do by first listening to learn what God would have us do and then attempting to carry it out.

True happiness lies in being fully engaged in what God wants us to do. We are often so certain that happiness lies in receiving what we desire. Surely that must include basic expectations like health, the necessities of life, and the love of others. The common notion of heaven on earth is thus equated with being happy because things are just as we would like them to be.

Many people feel that hell on earth is a condition where we are faced with terrible circumstances. Conditions are not minimally acceptable, and are certainly not part of an ideal state. Clearly, such a situation cannot be the way the world is supposed to be.

There is another perspective. The utter antithesis of contemporary culture, it seeks nothing more than alignment with God's will. Obedience is a term rarely considered in daily life, but it is at the heart of living a spiritual life. The sacramental acts of a single soul, longing for God and attempting to carry out what God wishes, elevate life to its most fulfilling level.

Many of us frequently seek distractions and comfort. We divert ourselves from the emptiness at the center of our lives with seemingly benign activities such as shopping, watching TV, and busyness, in the process consuming our time and thus our lives. If we seek comfort in such things as food or alcohol because our lives lack meaning, we create problems for ourselves. If our deepest, wordless self is empty, we will not be fulfilled by things of this world. Our souls long for a relationship with God and will not be satisfied with what we can touch and see.

It's difficult to let go of what we want, harder still to let go of what we need. But it is possible to reach through fear, suffering, and loss to grab hold of the hem of God's robe. If we do, our lives are suffused with mercy and we see the loving context of all that is.

What an irony it is to rip out and let go, to eliminate all those aspects of our lives that are not holy, purely for the love of God, only then finding that the gaps in our existence are filled with bliss. Not because we deserve it, not because we earned or expected it, but because we have aligned our lives with God's will.

We put tremendous effort into living life across the grain in an attempt to pursue our wants. If only we knew that a smaller effort, applied instead to seeking God's love, would be met with a flood of grace. A life attuned to that flood vibrates with joy.

What a marvel, to discover that heaven on earth is possible, even if for fleeting moments!

Calling

There is a great,
great river of pain.
I will not turn my back
nor stand on the bank,
comforting myself
with vicarious glance.
I must not stay dry -
moaning with pity.
I am called to wade in,
immerse myself.
Joining my drop of compassion
to dilute the flow.

Discussion Questions

1. The author, Michael Resman, describes his spiritual journey as it has unfolded through his career as a teacher of children in special education. How has your own work influenced your spiritual journey?
2. The author writes that the difficulties we face in our lives can bring blessings for ourselves and others. How have you been blessed by difficulties? Looking over your life, do you see God playing a role in bringing you difficulties or in resolving them, or both?
3. How have children [or those in need of your help] been teachers to you?
4. When people tell the author that he must have a lot of patience to work with severely disabled children, he replies that he has "appropriate expectations" [p. 5]. How is this insight helpful? Are there ways that "appropriate expectations" could be useful in your life or in the life of your meeting?
5. The author wrestles with a key theological question: if God is good, why is there so much suffering, especially suffering by innocent children? How do you respond to this question?
6. The author describes his "epiphany experiences"—his "direct experiences of God" which are "a form of mysticism" [p. 11]. These experiences are so strong that he is afraid others will question his sanity. How do you respond to Michael Resman's account of his mystical experiences? How would you describe your own spiritual experience? Can you identify with him when he says, "I no longer believed, I *knew* that God existed"?

7. How do you understand "heaven"? What does the author mean when he writes, "Our true, permanent home is heaven" [p. 13]? What are your reasons for agreeing or disagreeing?
8. The author finds religious meaning in the fact that some people have great needs, and he believes those of us who have much are called to give to those who have little. [See pp. 13–14.] How do you respond?
9. Do you agree with the author when he says, with reference to severely disabled children who suffer, "There is only justice in the next world . . ." [p. 14]. If this statement troubles you, why?
10. Have you had experiences similar to those the author describes "where in looking back, I can see that God has moved me here or there in order to make use of me" [p. 18]?
11. Have you ever struggled to forgive someone who has harmed you? What was your reason for wanting to forgive? Were you able to do so, and if so, what effects did it have?
12. For this author, much joy has resulted from service to others and from seeking to be obedient to God's will. Does his experience resonate with you? What experiences have you had of deep, spiritual joy, and what have you understood its source to be?